Silly Shakespeare for Students

PERICLES
PRINCE OF TYRE

PAUL LEONARD MURRAY

with help from

WILLIAM SHAKESPEARE

Alphabet PUBLISHING

I0379900

ISBN: 978-1-948492-73-7

Copyright 2020 by Paul Murray

All rights reserved. Our authors, editors, and designers work hard to develop original, high-quality content. Please respect their efforts and their rights under copyright law.

Do not copy, photocopy, or reproduce this book or any part of this book for use inside or outside the classroom, in commercial or non-commercial settings. It is also forbidden to copy, adapt, or reuse this book or any part of this book for use on websites, blogs, or third-party lesson-sharing websites.

For permission requests or discounts on class sets and bulk orders contact us at:

Alphabet Publishing
1204 Main Street #172
Branford, CT 06405 USA

info@alphabetpublishingbooks.com

www.alphabetpublishingbooks.com

For performance rights, please contact Paul Murray at paulplaying@gmail.com

Interior Formatting and Cover Design by Melissa Williams Design

This book is dedicated to the young people of the original
Belgrade English Language Theatre cast of
the play (2019) without whom it would have never been
written.

Marija Damnjanovič
Jana Dekanski
Eva Dragojević
Lea Harold
Cameron Howie
Martina Lakovič
Nikola Milutinovič
Marija Roganovič
Aisling Roth
Sinéad Roth
Anastasija Stojanovič
Sava Suvacarov

Summary

The original version of *Pericles* is generally regarded as being one of Shakespeare's weakest plays: indeed it was not included in the First Folio of his work as it was thought to be substandard. In his own day, however, the play was one of his most popular in theatres, presumably because there is so much action and so many opportunities for the dramatic.

***

Pericles, the Prince of Tyre, is in search of a wife. Following a visit to Princess A, our hero flees the island of Antioch because he discovers that Antiochus, the King of the island, is having an incestuous affair with his daughter. Pericles goes back to Tyre, but Antiochus sends an assassin to kill him. On the advice of his Lords, Pericles leaves Tyre in the care of his counsellor, Helicanus, and travels to Tarsus where his food supplies help Governor Cleon and his wife Dionyza prevent a famine. News reaches Pericles that an assassin is on his trail and so he sets sail once again, this time to Pentapolis, however, *en route* his ship is wrecked and he is the only survivor.

After being discovered by some fishermen, Pericles wins a jousting tournament where the prize is Thaisa, the beautiful daughter of King Simonides. They fall in love and Pericles marries her. After so much time away from home Pericles decides to return home. Thaisa is pregnant now, and on the way to Tyre a storm at sea brings about the birth of her child, whom Pericles calls Marina. Thaisa apparently dies in childbirth. The grieving Pericles seals her in a watertight coffin, puts a note inside, and throws the coffin in the sea.

The coffin floats and finally ends up on a beach in Ephesus. The local doctor/mystic Cerimon revives Thaisa. She mistakenly believes that Pericles has been lost at sea and is offered sanctuary in the Temple of Diana. In the meantime, Pericles has visited Tarsus and left Marina and her nanny Lychorida with Cleon and Dionyza who have agreed to raise her with their own daughter Philotene.

There is a fourteen-year gap in the action. Marina's nanny Lychorida has been killed by jealous daughter Philotene and Marina is now a beautiful young woman. Dionyza is also jealous of her and makes up her mind to have her killed. She instructs a servant/therapist Leonine to kill her but before she can Marina is captured by pirates. The servant escapes the pirates by hiding. After the kidnapping, Leonine tells Dionyza that she's killed her and has thrown the body out to sea. Dionyza orders a statue to be built in her honour (in case Pericles comes to visit).

When Pericles visits Tarsus he sees the statue and falls into a pit of despair. In the meantime the pirates have sold Marina to a brothel in Mytilene; however with her intellect and spirit she wins over the island's governor, Lysimachus and she is freed with her honour intact.

Pericles arrives in Mytilene and encounters Marina. They talk without at first knowing who each other is. After their conversation he soon recognises her and there is a joyful reunion. Lysimachus proposes to Marina and she accepts him. Pericles then has a dream in which he is instructed to go to Ephesus. He takes Marina with him. When they arrive, they meet Thaisa, who is now a nun, and the family is happily reunited. The baddies all die!

Playing Style

In this version of *Pericles*, the playing style is much more light-hearted than the original. This version of Shakespeare's 'worst play' lends itself to a clown/grotesque playing style. As such, it makes fun of all the different and sometimes controversial aspects (such as incest and prostitution) of the original. This playing style has its roots in Commedia dell'Arte and can be found most recently through the work of Jacques LeCoq or Fillipe Gualier or Peepolykus. In this particular style, the costumes are brash and props are minimal and created in a rough style (Peter Brook, *The Empty Space. The Reduced Shakespeare Company*).

What is also important about this style is that there is no fourth wall, which means the characters will very often talk directly to the audience, thus adding to the sense of fun and intimacy. On some occasions you will find the rhyming scheme helpful to the playing, in which case the actors should just 'stand back', enjoy the words, and help the audience do the same. On other occasions the rhyming scheme will seem stifling and restrictive, in which case do not be afraid to improvise a little, add your own occasional lines, or not emphasise the rhymes so much. Overall this version should be fun to play and watch, it can be produced with a small budget and should be 'over the top' to give you a chance to play with your own ideas of theatricality.

Staging

The staging of this version of the play is challenging but potentially very fun. It can be performed with a cast of 12 or more actors. (All actors in a cast of 12 will play multiple parts except for the actor playing Pericles). The narrator character Gower can be played by a number of actors. In the Final Act, Act V, some quick costume changes may be required for the brief appearances of King Antiochus, Princess A, Cleon, Dionyza, and Philotene if the actors playing them are also playing other roles in the scene.

Because of the quick scenes and the change scene locations I would recommend performing 'in the round' with a minimal set. Four rostra or tables can be placed as mini stages at stations on the edge of the playing circle, in between which four blocks of audience sit. The action takes place in each station and in the middle of the circle and surrounding each station. (N, S, E and W).

In the original production the staging was organised in the following way. The stage directions make reference to this layout to help give an idea of how the action could be organized.

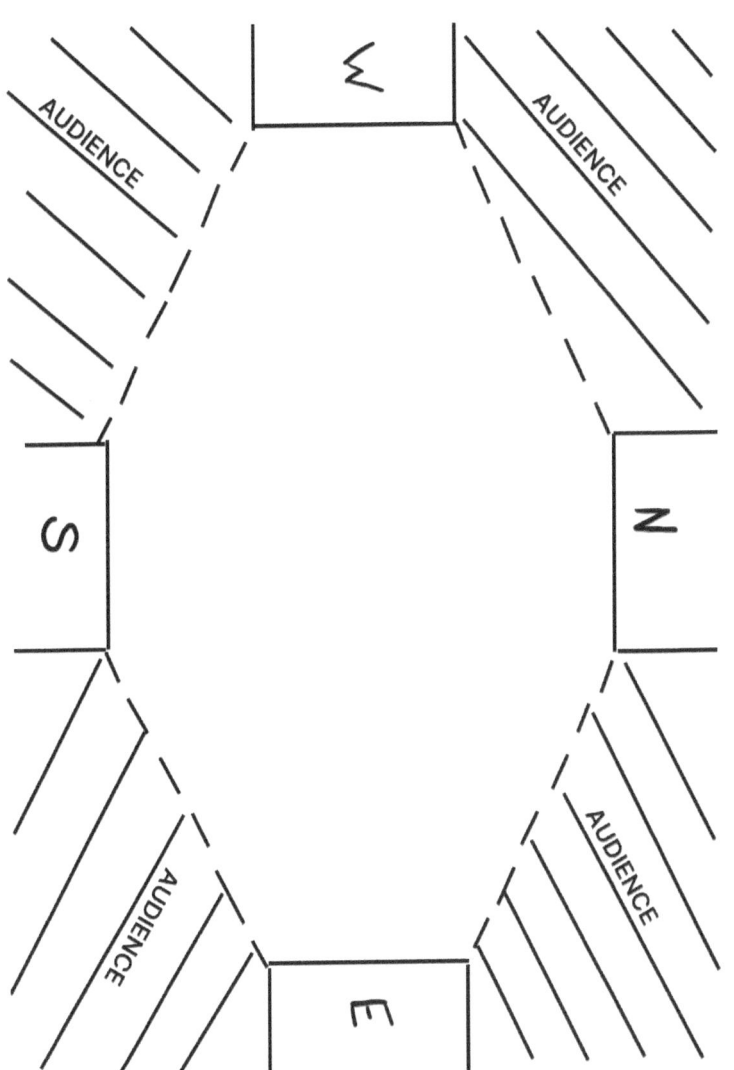

Cast of Characters

ACT I

GOWER:	the narrator
PERICLES:	Prince of Tyre
KING ANTIOCHUS	King of Antioch and father and in incestuous relationship with ...
PRINCESS A	
THALIARD:	Assassin sent from King Antiochus
HELICANUS:	Pericles' trusted advisor from Tyre
LORD 1:	from Tyre
LORD 2:	from Tyre
LORD 3:	from Tyre
LORD 4:	from Tyre
CLEON	Governor of Tarsus
DIONYZA:	Wife to the Governor of Tarsus
MESSENGER:	male, mistaken for a woman

ACT II

PERICLES	
BILL:	A local fisherman from Pentapolis
ANN:	A local fisherwoman from Pentapolis
SARAH:	A local fisherwoman from Pentapolis
COMMENTATOR 1:	an excited TV-style sports commentator from Pentapolis

COMMENTATOR 2:	an excited TV-style sports commentator from Pentapolis
SIR HARRY WHITE:	King Simonides' champion and favourite of Pentapolis
SIMONIDES	King of Pentapolis
THAISA:	King Simonides' daughter

ACT III

BABY MARINA:	Pericles and Thaisa's daughter
LYCHORIDA:	Marina's nanny
SAILOR 1:	One of Pericles' crew on The Glider
SAILOR 2:	One of Pericles' crew on The Glider
CERIMON:	Doctor and healer from Ephesus
CLEON	
DIONYZA	

ACT IV

MARINA	
DIONYZA	
PHILOTENE:	Cleon and Dionyza's daughter
LEONINE:	Servant/therapist
PIRATE 1	
PIRATE 2	
PIRATE 3	
BOULT:	Market trader, seller of young girls
PANDER:	Brothel owner's assistant
BAWD:	Brothel owner
LYSIMACHUS:	Governor of Mytilene
PERICLES	
HELICANUS	
CLEON	
MESSENGER	

ACT V

GOWER
PERICLES
THAISA
MARINA
HELICANUS
KING ANTIOCHUS
PRINCESS A
CLEON
DIONYZA
PHILOTENE
CERIMON
LYSIMACHUS
SAILOR 1
SAILOR 2
DIANA: *Ghost of the Goddess*
NUN 1:   *From the Temple of Diana, Ephesus*
NUN 2:   *From the Temple of Diana, Ephesus*

Act 1

Prologue

Enter GOWER *(This can be one actor centre stage delivering the monologue, or multiple actors each appearing in various locations taking a line or two)*

GOWER
You know the plays that Will did write
Macbeth, King Lear, Midsummer's night?
Othello, Hamlet, Much Ado?
Well these are but his favoured few.
Plenty more are seldom seen:
Henry the VIII and Cymbeline[1]
But bottom of the all-time list
Of Shakespeare's not-so-greatest hits
The play which always fails to please
The poor, unfortunate Pericles.
But before you stand and leave your seat
I have to say our play's a feat[2]
Of editing and derring-do[3]
To bring only the best to you

1—These are titles of plays by Shakespeare.

2—A great achievement

3— Act of bravery

In forty minutes, not one sec more,
Your jaws will be upon the floor.
Your senses will again regale[4]
From having viewed our glorious tale.
So sit back, relax, enjoy the night,
As Pericles comes into sight.

(PERICLES appears on stage)

To Antioch has our hero come
From Tyre, to find a little fun

(PRINCESS A and KING ANTIOCHUS appear at station W)

In the shape of lovely Princess A
But her dad King Antiochus gets to say
Just whom the princess gets to wed
And who shall share her bridal bed.
But daddy and daughter's history is dense
They know each other in the biblical sense.
But from her suitors[5] they wear a muzzle
And instead he sets them all a puzzle

(Cryptic clues are handed to the audience)

To protect his regal reputation
From all the tabloid speculation
Those who fail to solve the clue
Will lose their head, but those that do
Will turn their heels and take their flight

4—Be happy

5—Men who want to marry a woman

And run from their incestuous[6] plight.

> (PERICLES *screams and runs. A messenger appears and delivers a message to* KING ANTIOCHUS. *He reads it*)

ANTIOCHUS
What do you mean: Pericles has fled?
He should be staying here to wed,
My daughter (*stroke*) lover Princess A
She is waiting for her wedding day
And now he'll tell all waifs and strays
About our little incestuous ways.
Thaliard, my faithful knave.[7]

> (THALIARD *enters*)

THALIARD
Beside you Lord, from cradle to grave.

ANTIOCHUS
Just cut your sycophantic wheeze
And go and find Prince Pericles
Cross the sea to his land called Tyre

> (*Points to station E*)

And take his life . . .

6—Sex between family members

7—A servant

THALIARD
... Say no more, squire.[8]

(Exit THALIARD)

PRINCESS A
So we carry on, needless to say,
Keeping it in the family way?

ANTIOCHUS
Don't make me out to be the baddy.
Now come and tell me 'who's your Daddy'?

(Exeunt ANTIOCHUS and PRINCESS A)

8—(Here) a landowner

Scene I.

Tyre. A room in the palace.
(PERICLES finishing his report to four LORDS and HELICANUS who are standing at station E)

PERICLES
And that is how my journey ended,
Antiochus and his 'Queen' offended.

LORD 1
I wouldn't like to wear your boots.
Antioch is full of brutes.

LORD 2
I'll give you odds of nine to two
That one of them will murder you.

LORD 3
Not only that but landing here
They'll cut us all from ear . . .

(A mimed 'neck cutting' move is passed down the line of LORDS)

LORD 4
. . . To ear.

HELICANUS
Your lust for love and foreign booty
Has undermined your solemn duty.
As long as you stay here on Tyre
We will all be in the line of fire.

PERICLES
Oh Helicanus, of course you're right.
I will board my ship this very night.
And set a course for the isle of Tarsus
To save not mine, but all of our arses!

(PERICLES 'exits' to his boat, station N)

SCENE II.

Tyre. A small room in the palace.

(Enter THALIARD *in a swimsuit, goggles, and rubber ring/or small inflatable dinghy)*

THALIARD
Sorry to barge in unannounced,
But your King Pericles must be trounced.[9]

LORD 1
Sorry mate, you're just too late.
Prince Pericles has skipped his fate.

LORD 2
He's on his way to other shores

*(*THE LORDS *mime the following)*

With golden sails and silver oars.

THALIARD
That sounds like quite a fancy craft
And I've only got this crappy raft.

LORD 3
He'll lead you on a merry dance.

9—Punished

LORD 4
To kill him now, you have no chance!

THALIARD
When Antiochus hears I failed
To kill your king I'll be impaled.[10]
I dreamed a life of future bliss.
I don't deserve a fate like this.

LORD 4
He won't be happy with us either.

HALICANUS
Listen, people, take a breather.
Just tell your king he died at sea
In a monstrous storm he didn't see.
He'll never show up, he's far too scared,
And that way all our lives are spared!

THALIARD
Well if that's ok with all of you,
It sounds like just the thing to do.

LORD 1
Let's not mourn those now departed.

LORD 2
Let's just get this party started.

(Everyone but PERICLES *begins to party and enjoy themselves and dance offstage)*

10—Killed by something sharp like a stake or a sword

##

Tarsus. A room in the Governor's house.

GOWER

(Centre stage)

Not yet four scenes and already we see
Incest, treachery, debauchery
But have no fear; it will not stop.

(Indicating as speaking)

As Pericles takes another hop
Across the sea he's Tarsus-bound

(CLEON, DYONYZA, and locals form a frozen tableau at station E)

Where also things are not so sound.
They're going through an awful famine
Of which we'll hear their royals a'jammin'.

(CLEON, DYONYZA, and locals come to life ... the locals are very animatedly reacting)

DIONYZA
Oh Cleon, my man and head of State,
Tell me, why are our crops so late?
People dying of starvation.

This is no way to run a nation.

CLEON
Oh Dionyza, my Queen, my all,
It's not my fault that the rains don't fall.
Don't blame me that the sun don't shine.
That we don't have bread or cake...

DIONYZA
... or wine
Or beer or veg or stew!
Everybody's blaming you.

(Locals point at him)

All our food has gone to waste
Thanks to your expensive taste.
Our people now to get their fill
Do throw their babies on the grill.

CLEON
Why are you so 'glass-half-empty'?
You didn't care when we had plenty.
You don't give a hoot about their plight.
You just want fillet steak tonight.

DIONYZA
This isn't about some stupid steak.
The food better come for all our sake.
I've prayed to the gods to avoid consumption.[11]

11—Tuberculosis, a very serious illness.

(PERICLES *arrives unseen from station N*)

PERICLES
Sorry for the interruption.
I couldn't help but overhear.
King Pericles. I'm not from here.
My ship is harboured in your port
And on it I do wish for nought.

CLEON
You here to brag or point a finger?

PERICLES
No, I need a place to linger
For a while, you see I'm being chased
And I've got so much food it's going to waste.

DIONYZA
If we agree to let you stay
Will you send your food our way?

CLEON
If you do, then we will be
Indebted to you eternally.

PERICLES
Of course I will, my Lady and Lord
In return for only room and board.

DIONYZA
May we not offer something grander?

CLEON
Maybe an evening with my sister Miranda?

(A male MESSENGER *enters through the crowd standing on station E)*

MESSENGER
My lord?

PERICLES
Miranda?

MESSENGER
No, but I get that a lot.
I've just come with a message to move on the plot.

CLEON
Well, don't just stand there, spill the beans.
Tell us what your presence means.

MESSENGER
The message comes from *(trying to read)* Helic-Anus
Who says you'll face even more dangers,
Cos the assassin left Tyre not feeling so merry,
With a hangover he says is legendary.

DIONYZA
I do not like what this man does say
Quick! Leave us your food and run away.

(PERICLES quickly runs to N, picks up bags, hands them over, and returns to N)

PERICLES
Cleon, Dionyza, Miranda, adieu.

CLEON AND DIONYZA
We won't forget...

MESSENGER
...Miranda who?

Act II

Scene I.

(Enter GOWER *as all others but* PERICLES *exeunt)*

GOWER
And so we end Act I of V
Our hero, Pericles, still alive
But seemingly his luck is cursed
And a storm hit his ship making everything worse.

(The whole cast make storm sounds, run across the space for a few seconds, spraying some water on the audience. At the end of which PERICLES *is lying central and three anglers are at station W, fishing).*

As Act II begins, he's all washed up
On Pentapolis without his ship.
There we find him all covered in sand.
With anglers[12] Bill, Ann, and Sarah at hand.

*(*PERICLES, *lying wet)*

12—Fishermen

BILL

It must have been about this long. *(Holds his hands out as if measuring a fish)*

ANN

If he's like my husband, he's got that wrong!

SARAH

Why must men always exaggerate
About the size of their little best mate?

BILL

I'm talking about a fish I caught.

ANN

Of course you are; that's what we thought.

BILL

It was long and dark and big and fat.

(PERICLES sits up, as though caught on one of the anglers' hooks)

SARAH

Goodness gracious! What is that? *(Pointing at PERICLES)*

PERICLES

'That', *(Standing, brushing himself off)* my good woman, is the Prince of Tyre.
I know it's not exactly royal attire,
But between you and me I've had a bad day
And we're only on Act II of the play.

BILL
We are but simple fishing folk
But I knew you were royal before you spoke.

ANN
Even soaked like a rat, you reek of class.

SARAH
And there's no mistaking that right royal arse.

PERICLES
Well that's very nice of you to say
But I am not feeling very royal today.
My search for a wife began with such hope
and look at me now... *(Moves to E)*

BILL
... It's a slippery slope.

ANN

(Crossing to E)

Don't listen to him, he's a big hairy git.

SARAH

(Crossing to E)

You're twice the man he is...

ANN
... With ten times his wit.

SARAH
Wit enough to win a Miss,
The future queen of Pentapolis.

BILL
You talking about Thaisa . . . ?

ANN
. . . The one and the same.

SARAH
King Simonides' daughter is looking for a flame.

ANN
It's a jousting event where the winner takes all.

SARAH
And in this case, it's Thaisa you will take to the ball.

ANN
That Princess Thaisa's quite a kisser.

SARAH
You shouldn't get there late and miss her.

PERICLES
I'll leave you now with thanks and haste
Don't want this royal bod to go to waste.

(Exit PERICLES*)*

ANN
(Calling after him) Good luck to you . . .

SARAH
... We'll make a wish.

BILL
Shame he smells like rotten fish.

(Exeunt all)

Scene II.

(The Central space in an arena. COMMENTATORS *(N),* THAISA *and* SIMONIDES *(S), excited crowd surround* SIR HARRY *who is standing on station W.* PERICLES *and* SIR HARRY *mime riding horses, perhaps with broomsticks, and carry swords, perhaps cardboard or foam)*

COMMENTATOR 1
(arriving hurriedly) I've just got back from the urinal
To commentate on the jousting final.

COMMENTATOR 2
And just in time, here's our favourite knight,
Pentapolis' own: Sir Harry White.

(Cheers)

COMMENTATOR 1
And on the left, a gallant knave
Rescued from a watery grave.

*(*PERICLES *jumps triumphantly onto station E. Silence)*

THAISA
Oh Daddy, do we need a joust?

SIMONIDES
Of course we do, my little mouse.

THAISA
It's all just so uptight and swanky.

SIMONIDES
Oh just shut-up and drop your hanky.

(THASIA *comes to the centre of the space and drops her hanky,* HARRY *and* PERICLES *jump off their stations and ride their "horses" towards each other*)

COMMENTATOR 1
So here we go, the best of three.
Harry's the favourite here for me.

(*First joust run, Harry hits* PERICLES *on the head with his sword, and ends up in front at E. The crowd cheer and run to E*)

COMMENTATOR 2
Well that was close, a mighty blow
Our Harry's putting on quite a show.

COMMENTATOR 1

(PERICLES *recovering moves to W as he and* HARRY *both prepare for return run*)

But our stranger is ready for the second pass.

COMMENTATOR 2
And here we go . . .

(PERICLES and HARRY run at each other, PERICLES kicks HARRY on the bottom. HARRY goes down, PERICLES is back at E, the shocked crowd are unsure where to stand, they hover in the central area)

COMMENTATOR 1
... He's kicked his ass
That's got to hurt. The champs in pain
But he's man enough to go again

(HARRY and PERICLES prepare for the final run)

So hold your horses, sharpen your wits.

THAISA
Oh please let's just get on with this.

(PERICLES and HARRY run at each other one last time, slow motion fight and HARRY is beaten, the crowd are shocked)

COMMENTATOR 2
That's it, it's over, Harry's down
He'll never get to wear the crown
Instead it goes to ...

(PERICLES moves in front of THAISA)

SIMONIDES
... On your knees.*(PERICLES gets on his knees)*

THAISA
Who is this knight ... ?

(THAISA removes his helmet)

PERICLES
... It's Pericles!

(The crowd cheers and exits)

Act III

Prologue

(Enter GOWER. PERICLES stands arm in arm with THAISA, SIMONIDES in a tableau)

GOWER
Act III starts now, and with all of their lovin'
Thaisa and Peri've a bun in the oven[13]

(A baby doll is thrown to PERICLES who puts it up THAISA'S jumper)

And when Thaisa found out that her hubby's a king
She did the only decent thing
She grabbed their nanny Lychorida

(LYCHORIDA appears in the tableau)

And they set sail for Tyre on her dad's ship 'The Glider'

(SIMONIDES shows them all towards N which is now The Glider. Two sailors are helping them on board)

13—An expression that means pregnant

Now you probably already guessed what's brewing!
That a storm hits the ship and that's what's ensuing.

PERICLES
You've got to be kidding? I just got dry!

GOWER
It's only a drizzle, it will soon pass by.

SCENE I.

(As with Act I, the rest of the cast run across the stage for a few seconds making storm noises and spraying some water on the audience. The storm noises continue...)

SAILOR 1
I've been at sea for many a year
But this storm fills even me with fear.

SAILOR 2
Forget what the narrator said
This hurricane will have us dead.

LYCHORIDA
The waves are huge, the lightning's near,
I fear for all our lives out here.

THAISA
I'm thinking this storm isn't so mild.
This shouldn't be happening to your woman with child.
I'm feeling ill, do something quick.

SAILOR 1
Stand back, me lads, she's going to be sick.

LYCHORIDA
Quick, Pericles, she don't look swell

Her face is blue...

SAILOR 2
... her legs as well.

LYCHORIDA
And to make it worse...

(Freeze as a member of the cast walks calmly on stage and sprays a little water on THAISA. As they leave the stage the energy immediately returns...)

... her water's broke
She's having the baby; it isn't a joke.

SAILOR 2
Heave ho now, lads. Let's give her a twirl.

(THAISA lays down, LYCHORIDA and the sailors line up in front of her, one sailor in the centre space one in front of station W. LYCHORIDA pulls out the baby (doll) and throws behind her, over her head, as the character catches the baby they say their line)

SAILOR 1
The baby's out... *(Throws her)*

SAILOR 2
... It's Marina...! *(Throws the baby to PERICLES)*

PERICLES
(Briefly looking to check) ... A girl!
So all's ok at the end of the day.

(SAILORS *and* LYCHORIDA *return to the ship. In the meantime unnoticed* THAISA *has collapsed*)

LYCHORIDA
(*Noticing* THAISA) You spoke to soon, she's passed away.

PERICLES
(*After a brief check, the crew make a graveside tableau*) You may be gone, but I swear my bride
To always keep you by my side.

SAILOR 1

(*Moving into the central space*)

I hear the gods, they speak to me.
They say to . . .

(*Gods' voices from off stage chanting: Throw her in the sea, throw her in the sea . . . only sailor one can hear them*)

. . . throw her in the sea.
(*Still hearing the voices*) They say if we keep her body on deck,
We'll all go down . . .

PERICLES
. . . Oh what the heck.
Go fetch a box and stuff her inside

(SAILORS 1 *and* 2 *mime fetching a coffin and bring it in front of N*)

Then throw her off the starboard side.

LYCHORIDES
Such a shame, I hope she floats.

SAILOR 2

(Arriving with SAILOR 1 *holding a coffin)*

I hope she don't sink other boats.

PERICLES
I'll pop inside this little note
Just in case the box does float

(Passes the note via a sailor who puts it in THAISA'S *hand)*

Now raise it up and when I say
Just push her in . . . Now! That's the way.

*(*THAISA'S *body is carried or pushed into the coffin on the floor in the central area by the sailors and a blue sheet representing the sea is placed over it)*

LYCHORIDES
Goodbye my dear, and don't you fear
I'll keep your babe, Marina, near.

(The storm stops immediately)

SAILOR 1
Hooray! We're going to be OK.

LYCHORIDES
But I don't think that this babe should stay.

(Smelling the baby)

She needs dry land and fresh nappies, I think.

PERICLES
I agree with you. Let's get rid of her stink.

(Pointing at E)

We'll dump her off at Cleon's place.
They owe me a favour and it'll give us more space.

SAILOR 2
We sail for Tarsus. Turn her about
And let's hope for once the weather holds out.

(Exeunt all but THAISA *who lies under the sheet central)*

Scene II.

GOWER
And so they sail for Cleon's shores.
But what has happened to 'her indoors'?
Lying on the ocean floor?
Or washed up on some foreign shore?
It should be no surprise to you
That Shakespeare went for option two.
And sure enough her coffin's found
Lying on some sandy ground
In Ephesus (feeling less than perky),
A historical town in modern day Turkey.
Now when corpses were found, so tradition it went

(CERIMON *appears as a crazy doctor approaching the coffin*)

They were taken to doctor Cerimon's tent
And here he is now with Pericles's wife
About to get the surprise of his life.

(THAISA *is lying down as if dead.* CERIMON *is inspecting her to check if she's dead. Suddenly* THAISA *comes back to life...*)

THAISA
Hey! Watch where you're putting your hands, you quack

CERIMON
You nearly gave me a heart attack
I thought you were dead...

THAISA
...Oh did you, indeed?

(She rises, covered in seaweed)

What made you think that?

CERIMON
It was all the seaweed...

THAISA

(Looking at the sheet)

Was this my coffin? Washed up on shore?

CERIMON
Where did you come from...?

THAISA
...I'm really not sure.
I don't know my name, or my place, or my plight.

CERIMON
It must have been one hell of a night.

THAISA
The last thing I know I was lying in bed
And the next thing you're bringing me back from the
    dead.

CERIMON
Well I'm far too modest to claim such a feat
But don't worry too much about being discrete

>   *(Pointing to audience members as though they are the following)*

Tell my wife, tell my kids, or the king even better
And all of the gods...

THAISA
... Oh, look here's a letter.

>   *(Noticing the letter in her hand... hands it to* CERIMON*)*

CERIMON
It doesn't look too clear to me.
Looks like it was written while sailing at sea:
(reading) "To whom it may concern"... That's I!
"You've found the apple of my eye.
We sent her to the ocean deep
Following her permanent sleep.
You've got your hands upon this note
Which means the coffin it did float.
She is a catch in death as well as in life
Mother of one and Pericles' wife."

THAISA
That's it, that's what happened. I remember it well
I gave birth then I died in a terrible swell.
Now my husband is gone and my little babe too
And I would be dead if it wasn't for you.

CERIMON

It's true what they say 'worse things happen at sea'

But don't worry, my dear, you can stay here with me.

Well, when I say 'me', *(pointing to a small cross, lit by a torch being held by a cast member behind the audience)* I mean stay at the church.

St Diane's was made for girls left in the lurch.

It's the place on the hill with a cross on the spire.

THAISA

And there I'll abide till my time does expire.

> (CERIMON *waves of* THAISA *who heads towards the church.* CERIMON *exits)*

SCENE III.

Tarsus. A room in CLEON'S *house.*
CLEON *and* DIONYZA *are in a tableau at station W.*

GOWER
Of course we all know that Thaisa's mistaken

(PERICLES, LYCHORIDA, *and baby appear E)*

Her hubby and nurse, the baby they've taken
To Tarsus, to find a home for the mite.

CLEON
Pericles, the Prince. You did give us a fright.

LYCHORIDA
Is this the couple you said that would save her?

PERICLES
Yes. This is the pair who do owe me a favour
Well you certainly look all well fed and happy.

CLEON
All thanks to you Lord . . .

LYCHORIDA
. . . Now, can you change a nappy?

DIONYZA
Of course we can. Meet our own bundle of joy

(A baby is thrown on and caught by DIONYZA*)*

Philotene, a girl . . .

CLEON
. . . but I wanted a boy.

PERICLES
All the better, cos I've got to leave in a hurry
My people on Tyre are starting to worry
Her name is Marina, and this is her nurse.

(Pushes LYCHORIDA *across the space towards* CLEON *and* DIONYZA*)*

LYCHORIDA
A job that's a blessing; or is it a curse?

DIONYZA
And where, may I ask, is the Mum of this tot?

LYCHORIDA
She perished at sea when the storm hit our yacht.

(After giving the baby, LYCHORIDA *starts walking back to* PERICLES *who pushes her gently back)*

PERICLES
So no lengthy goodbyes, I'll just leave them with you
She'll just be a burden on the things I must do.

CLEON
Farewell then, sweet prince. Safe journey home.

DIONYZA
And Marina we'll raise just like one of our own.

(Exeunt all but PERICLES *who moves to E looking lonely)*

Act IV

Prologue

GOWER
And in the blink of an eye Act III does expire
You'll be glad to know Pericles made it to Tyre,
Where he took back his place on the rubbery throne
Shame though he had to sit there alone

    (PERICLES looks sorry for himself and then exits)

But I hear what you're thinking, *(to a member of the audience)* I hear you, my friend:
Is this Shakespeare epic ever to end?
Well, have no fear. We'll now pick up the pace

    (MARINA appears sitting in area E)

And 14 years later, how fair in the face
Is Marina. We see her, step-sister in tow

    (PHILOTENE appears sitting in area W)

But all is not well, as we now here will show.

    (DIONYZA appears sitting in area N)

Scene I.

DIONYZA
Now listen you two, I've about had enough
Of all of this whining, it's time to get tough.

PHILOTENE
Well no need to take out your anger on me
I've done nothing wrong, I'm as sweet as can be.

LEONINE

(Appearing and walking around the central area as talking)

Now that's not what I've heard, Philotene, my dear.
As your family therapist my job here is clear.
I offer to you all here a safe space to share.

PHILOTENE
Did you hear that, you cow . . . ?

LEONINE
. . . Philotene! Unfair!

PHILOTENE
Why are you shouting? You think that I'm mad?
She may look sweet and lovely, but Marina is bad.

MARINA
I feel guilty that I'm the more beautiful sort,
That my grades are much better in art and in sport,
And in science and maths and extracurricular,
But I've nothing against Philotene in particular.

LEONINE
Thanks for your sharing. Something to add,
Philotene? About your Mum or your Dad?

PHILOTENE
What a condescending pile of crap.
No-one would blame me if I gave you a slap.

LEONINE
Now calm down, Philotene. Don't go kicking her fanny.

PHILOTENE
There's no need for that, cos I murdered her Nanny.
Revenge is a dish that is best served cold.

MARINA
But she died when I was only seven years old

PHILOTENE
Yes. I learned to be evil very early in life
And had help from a friend in twisting the knife. *(Pointing towards* LEONINE*)*

LEONINE
(Cutting her off) Well thanks, Phil, for sharing, Mummy, something to add?

DIONYZA
Well, not really. I just think it's just ever so sad.

LEONINE
Well, I feel we've made headway so, same time next week?

DIONYZA
I feel like we are getting to the peace that we seek.

PHILOTENE
Come on, Mum, let's take our bow
And leave her. Leonine, take care now, you cow!

(Exeunt DIONYZA and PHILOTENE. MARINA joins LEONINE centre)

MARINA
I'm glad to say that they have gone,
I need a little one-to-one.

LEONINE
Well, actually that suits me too
(In a very civilized tone) Cos I am going to have to murder you.

(Pulls out a knife)

If you require a little time to pray,
Just go ahead. I've got all day.

MARINA
But why kill me? I can't construe[14] it.

14—Understand

LEONINE
I don't quite know. Your Mum said do it.

MARINA
So what about that therapist bit?
Was that a lie? . . .

LEONINE
. . . Well, most of it.

MARINA
I've always cared a lot for you.

LEONINE
But she pays my wages . . . what can I do?
I got the taste by helping your sister
To kill your nurse. Without me she'd have missed her.
Now hold still, my dear. This won't take a mo'.

(From nowhere three very stereotypical PIRATES *arrive on the edge of the space in a dramatic fashion and strike very pirate poses)*

SECOND PIRATE
Not so fast there, my lovely . . .

THIRD PIRATE
. . . The girl. Let her go.

FIRST PIRATE
Well, shivver me timbers. We're here just in time!

*(*LEONINE *runs and hides near one station)*

SECOND PIRATE
That's her, that's Marina, let's throw her a line!

(A rope is thrown to MARINA *who takes it and is pulled to the edge of the stage and 'safety')*

THIRD PIRATE
We're swashbuckling pirates; Marina we'll save.

FIRST PIRATE
Now make for the ship and catch the first wave.

*(*PIRATES *take* MARINA *away,* DIONYZA *enters and joins* LEONINE *who has slowly appeared again)*

DIONYZA
I guess by all the screams about
That Marina's light has been snuffed out.

LEONINE
Oh *(appearing and acting surprised)* yes . . . I mean, yes!
    She's gone alright
But she didn't go quietly. She put up a fight.

DIONYZA
She always was a feisty cat.
Now tell me: where's the body at?

LEONINE
(Obviously lying) Already gone . . . washed out to sea.

DIONYZA
I'll miss that girl so terribly.
Let's build a statue, raise it high.

LEONINE
In case her dad should happen by?

DIONYZA
Following her 'sad and sudden' *(sarcastically)* demise
It will make us look good in Pericles' eyes.

(DIONYZA exits)

LEONINE
(Turns to audience) What's the matter? You think she's not dead?
The pirates will use her to warm up their bed
And do all the bad stuff that pirates do best
And then let the fishes take care of the rest!

(Exits)

SCENE II.

GOWER
And so we leave this scene's torment
To find out where Marina went.
Well, good news and bad news both here we can tell:
The good news is she's safe and well.
Her mind and her body still in one piece
And delivered to a sweet little island in Greece.

(The cast sit centrally as though at a marketplace facing N.)

BOULT

(Places a rope around MARINA'S *hands)*

The bad news is on Mytilene
We sell young girls for things obscene.

GOWER
On this Greek isle it does transpire.[15]
She's moved from frying pan to fire.

BOULT
Ladies and gentlemen, step this way.
We've got a new girl in today,

15—Happen

Free from touch and all infection,
Ideal for your lady collection.

PANDER

(From area S)

You see that, boss? . . .

BAWD

(From area W)

. . . of course, you twit
I see her too . . .

PANDER
. . . she's pretty fit.

(Shouting over the crowd)

Now how much for the pretty filly?
20 drachmas[16] . . . ?

(Crowd reacts to the negotiations)

BOULT
. . . Don't be silly
Look at this beauty. You're taking the piss . . .

MARINA
Don't I get a say in this?

16—Greek money

BAWD

Did she speak...?

BOULT

(To MARINA *quietly)* ... Now listen, you bird
The rule around here is to be 'seen but not heard'
(To the crowd...) No, gents, you're mistaken... I won't tell you again.

BAWD

The last thing we need is a girl with a brain
Our guys are put off by a girl with a spiel.

PANDER

(Moving towards BOULT*)* I'll go up to thirty. Do we have a deal?

(Offering his hand)

BOULT

Well you're robbing me blind, but I'll give her for thirty.
If you save me a turn before she gets dirty!

(They shake hands on the deal. MARINA *is brought centre stage and a sheet thrown over her. She is now a statue. Exeunt all as though the market is closed as* GOWER *starts speaking)*

Scene III

GOWER
Well it doesn't look too good for our dear young Marina
And for 14 long years her dad hasn't seen her.

(DIONYZA, CLEON, *and* PHILOTINE *enter and form a tableau in area W*)

He thought she was safe with Dionyza and Cleon
So he stayed home in Tyre for what seemed like an eon.
But when in his diary, a space did arise

(PERICLES, HERICANUS, SAILORS 1 AND 2 *enter area N*)

He sailed off to Tarsus to give her a surprise.

(*On* PERICLES' *ship*)

PERICLES
Helicanus, the sea is as calm as meat stew.

HELICANUS
And lo, there is Tarsus just come into view.

(CLEON *and family 'come to life', a messenger enters in a panic*)

MESSENGER
Your majesties, sorry, I've just had a tip
One of my men has just seen a ship.

PHILOTENE
We're an island, you twerp. That is hardly big news.

CLEON
That's right, little pumpkin, and I love those new shoes.

DIONYZA
Wait a second. He looks like he's just seen a ghost.

MESSENGER
Cos it's Pericles, ma'am, approaching our coast.

(On PERICLES' ship)

HELICANUS
Did you tell them we're coming? Cleon and his flock?

PERICLES
No, I thought I'd surprise them when our ship it docks.
Let's pull in right there beside that big stone.

HELICANUS
And we'll find your Marina and take her straight home.

(PERICLES and HELICANUS arrive on one side of the statue, CLEON, DIONYZA, PHILOTENE, and LEONINE arrive on the other)

CLEON
King Pericles, pardon our worrying looks

But your arrival here's a turn up for the books.

DIONYZA
I wish you'd sent word you were coming to call
I would have laid on a band and a welcoming ball.

HELICANUS
Don't worry 'bout that now. Our feet're on the ground.
We're here for Marina? Is she around?

PHILOTENE
Well in a manner of speaking, she's right here, my Lord

(Pointing at the statue)

But now she's a statue . . .

DIONYZA
(Hesitantly) . . . She fell overboard.

PERICLES
She did what? . . .

DIONYZA
She is dead . . .

LEONINE
. . . It's a terrible blow.

CLEON
But don't look at me: I didn't know.

HELICANUS
And this rock is the 'statue' to which you refer?

PHILOTENE
Well yes, it's postmodern. It's what we prefer.

PERICLES
First my wife, now my daughter, what sick play is this?

HELICANUS
Let's sail back to Tyre, Lord, you're bound to be missed.

PERICLES
No I can't, my good slave ...

PHILOTENE
... He looks full of dread.

PERICLES
I will pledge myself mute and we'll sail round the Med.

LEONINE
I think that that's best, if it makes him feel better.

CLEON
And when you get back home you can send us a letter.

HELICANUS
Well look after the ... 'statue' we'll be on our way
Pericles, anything you want to say?

> (PERICLES *shakes his head and exits,*
> HELICANUS *follows him*)

LEONINE
It's a strange thing, his grief: partly fear, partly malice.

CLEON
Oh shut it, you phony! Let's get back to the palace.

(Exeunt CLEON, DIONYZA, PHILOTENE, *and* LEONINE.
Only the statue remains as GOWER *enters)*

Scene IV.

Mytilene. A street before the brothel.[17]

GOWER
So King Pericles' day goes from bad to much worse.
He's not living the dream; he is living a curse.
Which brings us back to Marina's plight

(Enter BAWD who takes the sheet off MARINA and tries to tidy her up)

On Mytilene preparing for 'opening night'.

(Exit GOWER)

PANDER
Is she all settled in for the opening tonight?

BAWD
Eventually, yes, but she put up a fight.

PANDER
I hope you didn't hurt her . . .

BAWD
. . . No, nothing like that

17—A place where prostitutes or sex workers can be found

It was more of an intellectual spat.

PANDER
Intellectual? With you? Well I bet that was short
Does she realize her body is here to be bought?
She doesn't have to like it. She's just playing a part.

BAWD
A prostitute's union, she said she would start.

PANDER
Well our governor ain't going to like that very much
Cos he likes all his girls to be freelance and stuff.
It stops them having any recourse
When they're murdered...

BAWD
... Or catch some disease...

PANDER
... Yes, of course.

(LYSIMACHUS enters)

BAWD
Well, talk of the devil and the devil appears.

(On seeing LYSIMACHUS, PANDER hurries MARINA into the brothel offstage)

LYSIMACHUS
I heard she's a stunner, is she still...?

PANDER
... Yes, she is.

LYSIMACHUS
Right. I'm going straight up then. The room at the back?

PANDER
Same room as normal ...

LYSIMACHUS
... Look after my hat.

(Exit LYSIMACHUS *passing* PANDER *and hands him his hat as he heads towards the brothel ... during the following we hear noises from the brothel ...)*

BAWD
It's nice; politicians and others in suits
Take time out to welcome our newest recruits.

PANDER
It's heart-warming to see them give of their best
To make the new girls feel just the same as the rest.

BAWD
I hope that this newbie don't upset his Grace
Like I said she is feisty and right in ya' face.

PANDER
Oh come now, fella, they all start that way
But after a week they all do what we say
In my bones I can feel that Marina's a hit
And she makes us a fortune when she takes off her kit.

(LYSIMACHUS *appearing satisfied from the brothel*)

BAWD
Lysimachus, my Lord, tell us how is Marina?
As we said, you're the first in the city who's 'seen' her.

LYSIMACHUS
She's a joy, she's a wonder, from her head to her toes
Words can't describe all the things that she knows.

PANDER
Same time tomorrow then, more of the same?

LYSIMACHUS
I will never set foot in a brothel again!

PANDER
I don't understand . . .

LYSIMACHUS
. . . We just talked . . .

BAWD
. . . About what?

LYSIMACHUS
Human rights, women's lib, child abuse and whatnot.

BAWD
That doesn't sound good, and where is she now?

LYSIMACHUS
She's coming with me . . .

(MARINA *appearing calm and smiling*)

PANDER
You ungrateful old cow.

LYSIMACHUS
I will pay for her freedom and then you won't reach her.

MARINA
I'll pursue a career as a primary school teacher
I'll teach the young girls about how to respect
Themselves and their bodies . . .

BAWD
. . . so you didn't have sex?

MARINA
Get your head around this, and it may cause you dizziness,
From today Mr Bawd that is none of your business.

(*Exeunt all*)

Act V

Scene I.

On PERICLES' *ship*

GOWER
And so we arrive at the final act: V
With the main man, his wife and their kid still alive
But there's 'living' and 'living' *(with emotion)* as someone once said
So how do we put this story to bed?
After all of these twists, I hope it's dramatic...
The end it begins in the East Adriatic.

(PERICLES, HELICANUS, SAILOR 1 *and* 2 *on the ship in the N area looking very miserable)*

After three months at sea, just a'floating around,
And not saying anything, not even a sound,
Pericles' ship is in need of supplies.
And guess where it stops? Mytilene...

(LYSIMACHUS *and* MARINA *appear as on a pedalo/paddle boat (S) both peddling toward* PERICLES)

LYSIMACHUS
... Surprise!
I saw your ship's flag from my office on shore
And it looked pretty fancy to me ...

SAILOR 1
... Say no more
Just pull yourself up on the rope and we'll see
If our King is willing to meet here with thee.

> (LYSIMACHUS *and* MARINA *take the rope and climb up to Pericles' ship*)

LYSIMACHUS

> (*Pointing towards the isle in the near distance from which they've come*)

Good sire, a warm welcome to our little isle.
He's looking unhappy. C'mon, give us a smile.

HELICANUS
I'm afraid he will not. He has not said a peep
Since he found out his only daughter's 'asleep'.

SAILOR 1
After all he'd been through, what with losing his wife.

SAILOR 2
No human has had such a terrible life.

LYSIMACHUS
Well pardon me, gents, but I know of one maid
Whose story can rival the one that you've said.

She came to this isle for money exchanged
But our values and dreams she has rearranged.
She does not know your man, and don't say a thing.
I think she'd be shy if she knew he's a king.
But if anyone can help, it's this young girl . . . my dear?

(Gestures and MARINA *approaches)*

HELICANUS
Let's give them some space and wait over here.

(They wait a very short distance away)

GOWER

(As Marina mimes)

Marina, she did take a pew.
And told the king of all that she knew.
She hoped by telling him her woes
It would help to get back on his toes.
But something strange: on hearing her tale
A set of questions he started to rale.

PERICLES

(Starts walking around the central stage thinking, as though a detective or lawyer. He could visit the areas on stage where the events being reported took place)

Place of birth . . . ?

MARINA
. . . A ship at sea.

My mum died in delivery.

PERICLES
Your dad . . . ?

MARINA
. . . He left me with a nurse.

PERICLES
On an island . . . ?

MARINA
. . . It gets worse.
The island's queen she killed nanny
And then she tried to murder me.

PERICLES
Did she succeed . . . ?

MARINA
. . . a stupid question.

PERICLES
But it was her, the queen's suggestion?

MARINA
Her servant tried to slit my throat,
But I ended up on a pirate's boat.

PERICLES
From frying pan to fiery cooker.

MARINA
Then they sold me as a hooker.

PERICLES
They put you to work in that place so depraved?

MARINA
Yes, but from there I was rescued, and my honour was saved
By the man Lysimachus who's waiting outside.
He'd make a good husband...

PERICLES
... You'd make a good bride.

MARINA
Well you certainly seem like you're coming along.

PERICLES
I'm beginning to think something weird's going on.
The name of your nurse?...

MARINA
... Lychorida was she.
And Thaisa's the woman who gave birth to me.

PERICLES
And the name of your father? Tell me that, if you please.

MARINA
Well according to Nanny, he was called *(a dramatic pause can be added here as she tries to remember)* Pericles.

PERICLES
Merciful heavens, Lysimachus, come here.
What's the name of this beautiful dear?

LYSIMACHUS

Well I don't know her last name, but her first name's Marina.

PERICLES

Well then, she is my daughter. It's the first time I've seen her.

MARINA

You're really my father? . . .

LYSIMACHUS

. . . I don't comprehend.

SAILOR 1

She's the princess of Tyre . . .

LYSIMACHUS

. . . Thank you, my friend.

(Exeunt all apart from PERICLES *and* MARINA; *he sleeps with his head on her lap as* GOWER *enters)*

Scene II.

GOWER
With the King and his daughter together once more
You may think that this story has nothing left in store
But those of you paying closest attention

(THAISA *appears dressed as a nun miming the following (E)*)

Will remember that Thaisa was left in detention
In a temple for years, weeks, days and hours
Just worshipping Gods and watering flowers
So how do we end? I would be delighted
If we could somehow get these two birds reunited
But both think the other resides with the Gods
Reacquaintment would defy all the odds
It would take a plot twist of miraculous sorts
But Shakespeare, being Shakespeare, thought of something of course!

(DIANA *the goddess appears on high (W) to* PERICLES *in a dream. The rest of the cast are a heavenly chorus*)

DIANA
Do not wake, gentle mortal. Do not cry out or scream
I'm the Goddess Diana and I come to your dream.
I am glad that Marina was found on your route.

But you need to thank me for your hunt bearing fruit.
Now head off to Ephesus, my church on the hill.
Take your daughter and friends cos you'll need them all still.
At the altar stand tall, wear a tie and a blazer,
And explain how you came to lose Marina's mum, Thaisa.

(DIANA *remains in place*)

SCENE III.

GOWER
So in the final throw of Pericles' dice
They boarded his ship . . .

*(HELICANUS, LYSIMACHUS, SAILOR 1 and 2 join
PERICLES and MARINA)*

ALL THE ABOVE
. . . We didn't think twice.

GOWER
And before you could say . . .

ALL THE ABOVE
(said very quickly) Act Five scene Three

GOWER
They're stood in the temple . . .

PERICLES

(Moving from the ship to stand in front of DIANA)

. . . My buddies and me.

MARINA

> *(Moving to stand behind PERICLES)*

Marina, his daughter...

LYSIMACHUS

> *(Moving to stand with MARINA)*

...Lysimachus, her beau...

HELICANUS

> *(Moving to stand behind MARINA and LYSIMACHUS)*

Helicanus, his besty...

GOWER

...Were all there in tow
And the good doctor Cerimon...

CERIMON

> *(Joining the line at the back between W and E)*

...I love a good ending.

NUNS

> *(Joining THAISA (W))*

And a murmur of Nuns, to heaven ascending.

GOWER

> *(PERICLES miming his story to the crowd very quickly)*

So he told of his story, once again from the start

From the top of his head, cos he knew it by heart
We'll skip to the end just to finish the play:

PERICLES
... and that's how I came to stand here today.

(THAISA, *dressed as a nun, faints*)

NUN 1
At that moment one nun (who had not yet been sainted)

NUN 2
On hearing the story, fell over ...

CERIMON
... she's fainted.

NUN 1
Is she sick? Is she tired?

CERIMON

(*Moves to her*)

I've got time to appraise 'er
She fainted my dear ...

(*Pulling back her hood and lifting her head to reveal*)

... and this here is Thaisa.

(*General surprise*)

MARINA

(*Running to* THAISA)

That's my mum...

PERICLES
(*Running to* THAISA) ... That's my wife...

THAISA
(*Recovered, hugging* PERICLES *and* MARINA) ... We are all reunited.

GOWER
And our play's almost done...

ALL
... We are highly delighted.

(DIANA *steps down from her position and exits with all except* GOWER, PERICLES, THAISA, MARINA, LYSIMACHUS)

GOWER
So just a quick recap, to get it all clear
And then you can sod off and go get a beer.

PERICLES/THAISA
(*From (W)*) The King and his Queen, well, they did retire.

MARINA/LYSIMACHUS
        (MARINA *and* LYSIMACHUS *from E*)
And Marina with hubby ruled long back in Tyre.

(*Enter* ANTIOCHUS *and* PRINCESS A *speaking to audience*)

ANTIOCHUS
And King Antiochus, whose incest had once seemed so

frightening?

PRINCESS A
He and his princess were killed . . .

ANTIOCHUS/PRINCESS A
. . . struck by lightning. *(A flash and they die)*

(Enter CLEON *speaking to audience)*

CLEON
And Cleon . . . ?

(Enter DIONYZA *speaking to audience)*

DIONYZA
. . . His wife . . . ?

(Enter PHILOTENE *speaking to audience)*

PHILOTENE
. . . And their sweet Philotene?

LYSIMACHUS
Who failed in their bid to kill off my Marina?

PHILOTENE
When the Thasians found out how evil we'd been

DIONYZA
They set fire to our house . . .

CLEON/PHILOTENE
. . . And cooked us with the Queen. *(They scream quickly*

and fall dead)

GOWER
So 'all's well that ends well' as Willie once said.
The good guys all win, and the bad guys are dead.
And that's pretty much it, for William's worst play.
And we'll end with a song . . . the traditional way.

> (THE CAST *gather for in centre to sing and dance the following, to the tune of "The Bare Necessities")*

Now go and be like Pericles
Our simple hero Pericles
Forget about your island and your wife.
I mean like, be like Pericles
A man who likes to sail the seas
And bring the play of Pericles to life.
If you want to be Hamlet,
Or Henry Part II,
Or even be Macbeth
That's much a do
The scholars all denounce this play
And think they have the final say
But if you look under their prejudice
And take a glance at his tasty bits
And maybe try a few . . .
The play of Pericles, in life, will come to you
Will come to you.

More Drama Resources from Alphabet Publishing

Silly Shakespeare for Students by Paul Leonard Murray

A Midsummer Night's Dream

Macbeth

Short Original Plays by Alice Savage

Just Desserts: A foodie drama about a chef gone bad

Introducing Rob: Lola's family loves her new boyfriend. Until they actually meet him

Colorado Ghost Story: Two exchange students get into trouble in the old West

Strange Medicine: Who decides what the truth is?

The Drama Book: Lesson Plans, Activities, and Scripts for the English Language Classroom by Alice Savage

ISTD Coursebooks by Alice Savage

The Integrated Skills Through Drama coursebooks contain a complete curriculum built around an original one-act play. Aimed at intermediate learners, teenagers and older.

Her Own Worst Enemy: A serious comedy about choosing a major

Only the Best Intentions: A love triangle between a guy, a girl and a game

Rising Water: A stormy drama about what happens to people in a crisis

Alphabet Publishing is an independent publisher of creative and innovative educational material. All of our resources were conceived and created by teachers working in the classroom. We support our creators by giving them creative control and by sharing profits. Learn more about us and our resources at www.alphabetpublish.com

www.ingramcontent.com/pod-product-compliance
Lightning Source LLC
Chambersburg PA
CBHW030159100526
44592CB00009B/353